Deathwatch

Robb White

TEACHER GUIDE

NOTE:

The trade book edition of the novel used to prepare this guide is found in the Novel Units catalog and on the Novel Units website. Using other editions may have varied page references.

Please note: We have assigned Interest Levels based on our knowledge of the themes and ideas of the books included in the Novel Units sets, however, please assess the appropriateness of this novel or trade book for the age level and maturity of your students prior to reading with them. You know your students best!

ISBN 978-1-56137-140-2

Printed in the United States of America.

To order, contact your local school supply store, or:

Toll-Free Fax: 877.716.7272
Phone: 888.650.4224
3901 Union Blvd., Suite 155
St. Louis, MO 63115

sales@novelunits.com

novelunits.com

Table of Contents

Skills and Strategies

Thinking
Brainstorming, mapping, visualization, research, problem solving

Comprehension
Predicting, comparison/contrast

Writing
Poetry, journaling, titling, descriptive

Vocabulary
Analogies

Listening/Speaking
Discussion, debate

Literary Elements
Characterization, story elements, similes, metaphors, personification, symbols, foreshadowing

Summary

Ben, a young man familiar with the desert, has been hired as a guide by Madec, a businessman anxious to bag a bighorn sheep. When an old prospector is accidentally shot, Ben and Madec disagree on the right thing to do. When Ben refuses Madec's proposal, he finds himself the hunted one. Ben is forced to make his way across the desert with no clothes, no food, no water. A maniac with a gun tracks him.

Pre-reading Discussion

1. What might the title mean?
2. The cover of the book shows a desert scene. Have you ever visited a desert? What are some characteristics of a desert?
3. Read the sentence on the cover. If you were in that situation, what chance would you have to escape? How would you do it?
4. This book does not have chapter titles. As you read, write a title for each chapter in your journal or notebook.
5. If you were marooned in the desert, which of the following would you need the most? Arrange the list of items in order of importance.
   a) Food
   b) Water
   c) Hat
   d) Jacket
   e) Shirt
   f) Shoes
   g) Socks
   h) Trousers
   i) Sunglasses
   j) Gun
   k) Jeep
   l) Compass
   m) Radio

   Be ready to defend your arrangement. *(Answers may vary.)* This assignment could be discussed in small groups.

Introductory Activities

Teachers are encouraged to adapt the Novel Unit to meet the needs of individual classes and students. You know your students best; we are offering you some tools for working with them. Here are some of the "nuts and bolts" for using these "tools"—a glossary of some of the terms that will facilitate your use of this guide.

Bloom's Taxonomy: A classification system for various levels of thinking. Questions keyed to these levels may be:

- Comprehension questions, which ask one to state the meaning of what is written;
- Application questions, which ask one to think about relationships between ideas such as cause/effect;
- Evaluation questions, which ask one to judge the accuracy of ideas;
- Synthesis questions, which ask one to develop a product by integrating the ideas in the text with ideas of one's own.

Graphic Organizers: Visual representations of how ideas are related to each other. These "pictures"—including Venn diagrams, flow charts, attribute webs, etc.—help students collect information, make interpretations, solve problems, devise plans, and become aware of how they think.

Cooperative Learning: Learning activities in which groups of two or more students collaborate. There is compelling research evidence that integration of social activities into the learning process—such as small group discussion, group editing, group art projects—often leads to richer, more long-lasting learning.

This book will be read one chapter at a time, using DRTA (Directed Reading Thinking Activity) Method. This technique involves reading a section, predicting what will happen next, making good guesses based on what has already occurred in the story. The students continue to read and everyone verifies the predictions. (See pages 5-6 of this guide.)

Before reading, specific vocabulary words will be pointed out. Students may write simple definitions in their own words before reading. After reading, ask students to redefine the words referring to the context or dictionary.

After reading a chapter, brainstorm "what ifs." What if one or another character wasn't in the story, a character did something different, events followed a different sequence or didn't happen at all, etc. The teacher writes all these "what if" class responses on the board or large sheet of paper. At the conclusion of the novel, the review of these "what ifs" may be used in writing a different development and/or ending for the novel.

Using Predictions in the Novel Unit Approach

We all make predictions as we read—little guesses about what will happen next, how the conflict will be resolved, which details given by the author will be important to the plot, which details will help to fill in our sense of a character. Students should be encouraged to predict, to make sensible guesses.

As students work on predictions, these discussion questions can be used to guide them: What are some of the ways to predict? What is the process of a sophisticated reader's thinking and predicting? What clues does an author give us to help us in making our predictions? Why are some predictions more likely than others?

A prediction chart is for students to record their predictions. As each subsequent chapter is discussed, you can review and correct previous predictions. This procedure serves to focus on predictions and to review the stories.

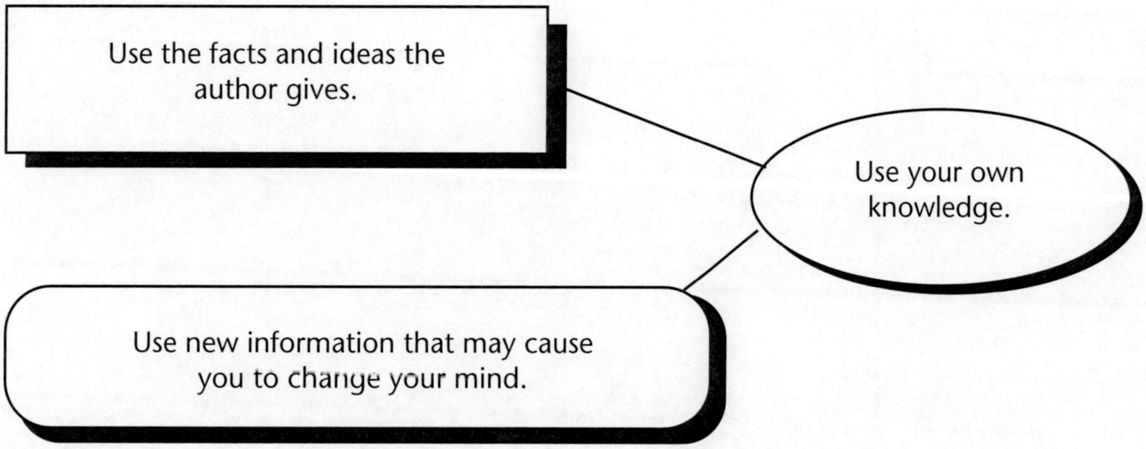

Use the facts and ideas the author gives.

Use your own knowledge.

Use new information that may cause you to change your mind.

Predictions:

____

____

____

____

Prediction Chart

What characters have we met so far?	What is the conflict in the story?	What are your predictions?	Why did you make those predictions?

Story Map

Setting

Problem

Goal

Episodes

Resolution

Characters____

Time and Place____

Problem____

Goal____

Beginning → Development → Outcome

Resolution____

Using Character Webs in the Novel Unit Approach

Attribute Webs are simply visual representations of characters from the novel. They provide a systematic way for the students to organize and recap the information they have about a particular character. An attribute web may be used after reading the novel to recapitulate information about a particular character or completed gradually as information unfolds, done individually, or finished as a group project.

One type of character attribute web uses these divisions:

- How a character acts and feels. (How does the character act? How do you think the character feels? How would you feel if this happened to you?)
- How a character looks. (Close your eyes and picture the character. Describe him/her to me.)
- Where a character lives. (Where and when does the character live?)
- How others feel about the character. (How does another specific character feel about our character?)

In group discussion about the student attribute webs and specific characters, the teacher can ask for backup proof from the novel. You can also include inferential thinking.

Attribute webs need not be confined to characters. They may also be used to organize information about a concept, object or place.

Attribute Web

The attribute web below is designed to help you gather clues the author provides about what a character is like. Fill in the blanks with words and phrases which tell how the character acts and looks, as well as what the character says and what others say about him or her.

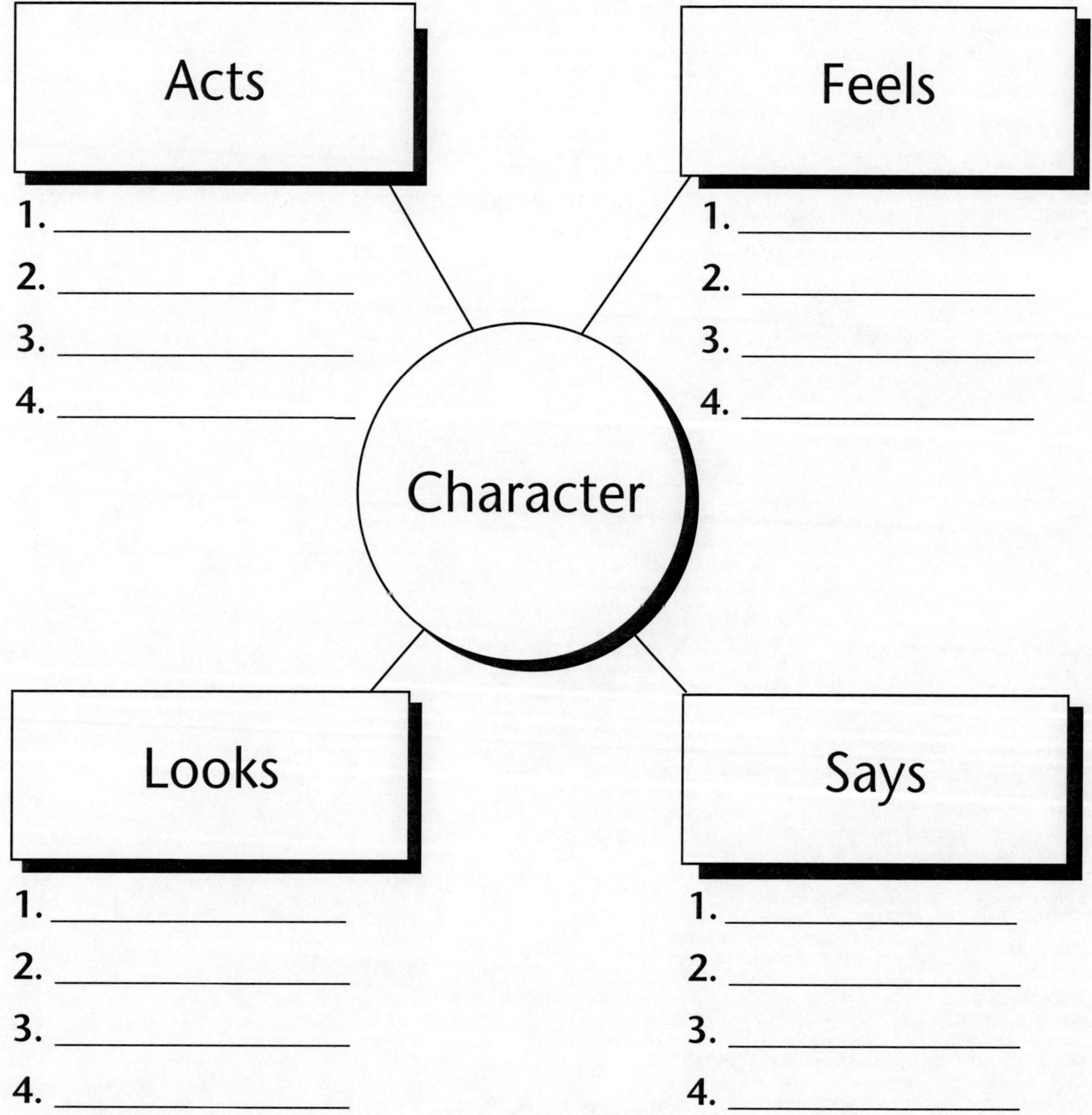

Attribute Web

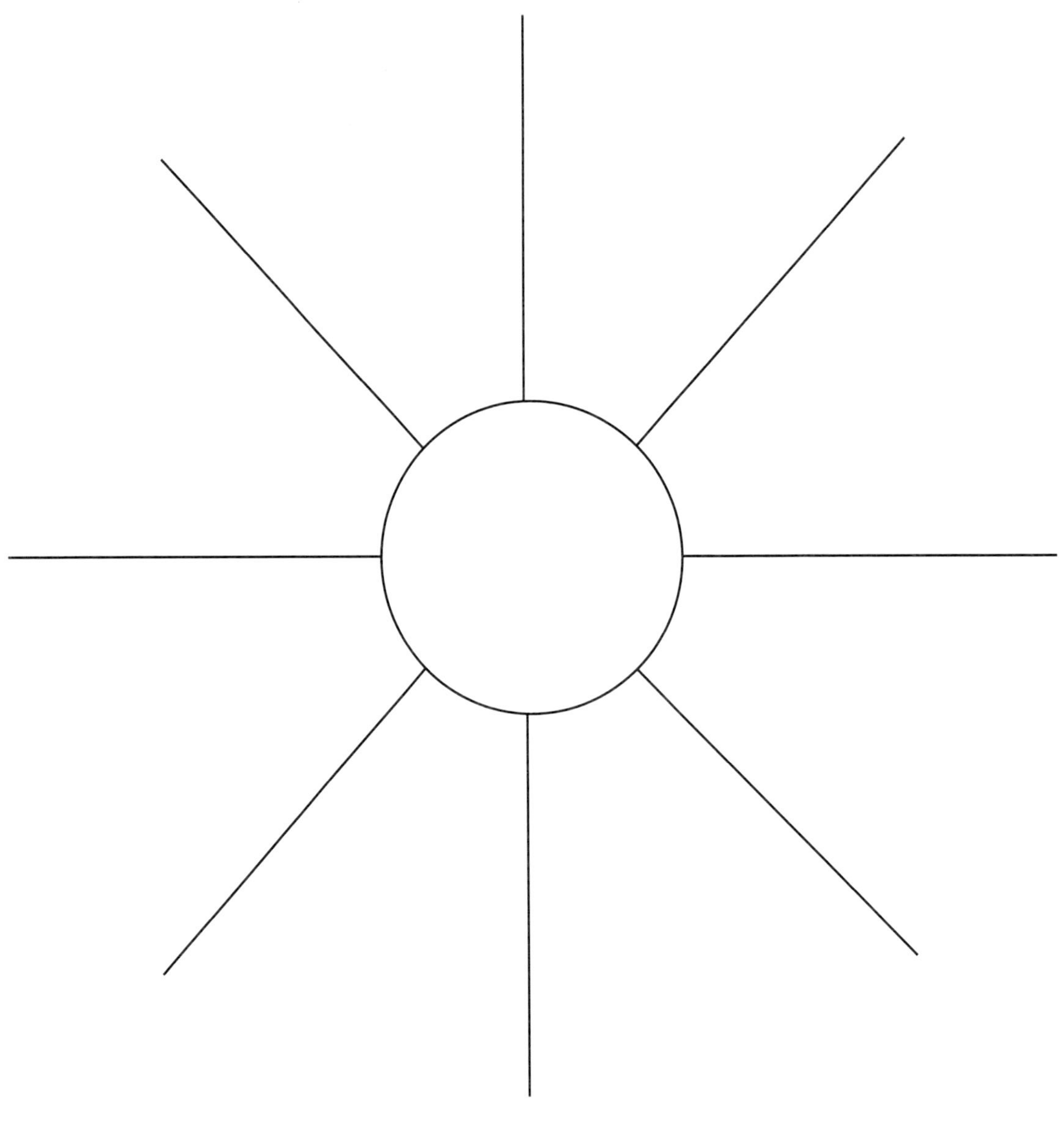

Chapter 1—Pages 9-19

Vocabulary

wariest (11) shale (16) congealing (18) fissure (19)

Discussion Questions and Activities

1. What do we learn about Madec's character in the first chapter? Make an attribute web to organize your thoughts on Madec. (See page 10 of this guide.) *(Answers may include: Page10, dangerous with gun, cold, intense, proud [wants to mount head of sheep in office]; pages 10-11, good shot; page 12, enjoys hurting people; page 17, liar.)*
2. What might this sentence mean? "It was the look of murder"—page 10. *(Answers will vary.)*
3. Differences between Ben and Madec show up immediately in the book. Chart the differences in Chapter 1. Include their attitudes towards hunting, especially hunting the bighorn, and towards money.

Ben	Madec
Wouldn't really want to kill a bighorn	Obsessed with the idea of killing a bighorn
Hunted for food	Hunted for accomplishment
Needed money	Rich

Supplementary Activities

1. Have you ever done any hunting? What were you hunting? Where? With whom? Write a short paragraph describing either the joys of hunting, why you think you would enjoy hunting, or why you are against hunting as a sport.
2. Where does the story take place? What are some of the clues? *(Edwards Air Force Base)*
3. **Prediction:** Who do you think the "white-haired man" is?

Chapter 2—Pages 20-30

Vocabulary

ewe (21) trajectory (24) velocity (24) derelict (27)

Discussion Questions and Activities

1. What is the old man doing in the hills? *(Page 20, He has a metal locator; page 21, a prospector; page 22, just to be by himself.)*
2. What does Madec propose to Ben? *(Pages 28-29, Madec offers Ben money for college and the promise of a job in exchange for keeping quiet about the old man's death.)* Would most people have reacted the way Ben does to Madec's proposal? *(Answers vary.)*
3. How does the old man get shot twice? Add more differences to your chart.

Ben	Madec
Compassionate	Hard-hearted

Supplementary Activities

1. Should Ben have accepted Madec's proposal? Would most 19-year-olds? Would you? Is Madec's argument logical?
2. The old prospector enjoyed his life alone. Do you enjoy being alone? Write a paragraph about a time you enjoyed being alone or describing a place you like to go to be alone.
3. Write a poem about loneliness or solitude. Is there a difference?
4. **Prediction:** Why would Madec shoot the old man twice?

Chapter 3—Pages 31-42

Vocabulary

contingency (33) perjure (34) arroyo (41)

Vocabulary Activities

1. Use the vocabulary words from Chapters 1-3 to answer these questions:
   a) What else besides a bullet would have both **velocity** and a **trajectory**?
   b) Could you find a **fissure** in **shale**?
   c) Give an example of a time when you might be **wary**.
2. Analogies: An analogy compares two things and shows the relationship between them. Example: May : spring—October : __________ *(autumn)*
   a) Fruit : strawberry—rock : __________ (kind of)
   b) Chicken : hen—sheep : __________ (female of)
   c) Family : orphan—money : __________ (lacking in)
   d) Shoplift : steal—lie : __________ (synonym)

(Answers: a) shale; b) ewe; c) derelict; d) perjure)

Discussion Questions and Activities

1. How does Madec explain his idea of a "contingency"? *(Page 33, Madec calls the second shooting of the man a "contingency," something that may or may not come in handy later.)*
2. On page 40 Madec explains why he is a more important person than Ben. Do you agree with his reasons? Does Ben seem like a "loser"? *(Answers will vary.)*
3. In your journal or notebook, write titles for the first three chapters.

Supplementary Activities

1. Madec and Ben compare people in small towns with those in big cities. Which do you prefer? If you could live anywhere you wish, where would you choose? Write a paragraph about your favorite place in the world to live. Be as specific as you can. Your spot may be real or imaginary. Be sure to give reasons. (If students have a journal, this assignment could be written in the journal. After several writing assignments, students might pick one journal entry to revise and proofread.)
2. **Prediction:** Will Ben be able to get the old man's boots?

Chapter 4—Pages 43-55

Vocabulary

lee (47)	collateral (48)	jerry can (49)	suffusing (51)
alien (51)	mesquite (53)	formidable (53)	

Discussion Questions and Activities

1. Give some examples of Madec's cleverness/intelligence. *(Page 46, He takes the old man's rope, blanket, boots; page 49, he finds and destroys the old man's camp.)*
2. How does the incident with the watering can emphasize Madec's cruelty? *(Page 50, He has smashed the bottom of the can but put it back in its hiding place.)*
3. How does the paragraph about the stars (page 51) reflect Ben's feelings? *(The stars had seemed close and friendly; now they are cold, distant, and unconcerned.)*
4. What does Ben find in the old man's box? *(page 53, a slingshot)* How might this be useful? *(page 54, to kill food and to use as a weapon)*
5. Why does Ben leave the other things in the old man's tin box? *(page 55, so someone else might find them)* Why?
6. Figures of Speech—Similes and Metaphors: A simile is a figure of speech in which a comparison is made using the word *like* or *as*. A metaphor is a figure of speech in which a comparison is made without using the word *like* or *as*.
   a) Find a metaphor on page 20. How can teeth be like fangs?
   b) Find two similes on page 43. How are mountains like coal and also like a pile of lettuce?
   c) Find a simile on page 45. Explain the comparison. *(headlight beams—knifeblade)*
7. Figure of Speech—Personification: Personification is the giving of human qualities to something nonhuman, such as an animal, an object, or an idea.
   a) Find an example of personification on page 47. *(moon—shy and undecided)*
   b) On page 51, how are the stars described? *(friendly, hostile)* How is this an example of personification?

Supplementary Activities

1. Have you ever been lost in the woods or had some similar frightening experience that required physical courage? Write a paragraph about this experience. Be sure to include words and phrases that describe your feelings during that time.
2. **Prediction:** Where might Ben find water?

Chapter 5—Pages 56-67

Vocabulary

foreboding (56)	lacerated (58)	tremor (61)	quartz (61)
preened (62)	butte (62)	panorama (62)	tenacious (63)

Vocabulary Activity

Replace the bolded part of the sentence with a vocabulary word from Chapter 4 or 5.

1. As Sammy stepped into the dark alley, he felt a sense of **fear**.
2. When the toddler tumbled down the stairs, she suffered **bruises** and cuts.
3. Jackie's dog had a **stubborn** hold on the bone.
4. Dad always adds some **wood shavings** to his charcoal.
5. Try to pitch your tent on the side **away from the wind**.
6. With so many .300 hitters, the Cougars were opponents **that aroused fear**.
7. Our slides showed only one bit of the mountainside, not the entire **view**.
8. The smell of the burnt potatoes **spread throughout** the apartment.
9. The Watsons were refused a bank loan because they had no **security**.
10. After Grandpa's stroke, his hand suffered from a slight **shaking**.
    (Answers: 1. foreboding; 2. lacerations; 3. tenacious; 4. mesquite; 5. lee; 6. formidable; 7. panorama; 8. suffused; 9. collateral; 10. tremor)

Discussion Questions and Activities

1. How does Ben explain the difference between fear and foreboding? *(Page 56, Fear is the paralyzing feeling Ben has when he expects Madec to shoot him. Foreboding is the dark, paralyzing fear of something about to happen.)* Could you give other examples of both?
2. On page 60 Ben wonders if Madec would deliberately shoot him. Would he? Why or why not?
3. Why doesn't Ben go north, away from Madec? *(Page 63, He has no water, no food, no clothes. He could never walk 100 miles in that condition.)*
4. Find Ben's three choices. *(Page 64, a. stay where he is; b. start walking 65 miles east; c. walk 35 miles west.)* Which seems like the best one to you?
5. On page 65 the author notes, "Mechanics, machines, supplies were not a part of this game. In the final analysis, even the guns were not a part of it." What does he mean? What **will** determine the winner of this deadly "game"? *(Answers will vary.)*
6. Add more differences to your chart of Ben and Madec. *(Examples, page 66, Madec is vain, conceited, and sure of himself.)*

Supplementary Activities

1. Draw a map. Label the directions **N, S, E, W**. Label the distances Ben must walk in each direction. Label the positions of Ben, Madec, the small mountains, the butte, the high mountains.
2. **Prediction:** Will Ben be able to get to the catch basin for water?

Chapter 6—Pages 68-80

Vocabulary

crag (70)	magma (72)	basalt (72)	pumice (72)
breccia (73)	pinnacle (73)	mesas (74)	sentinels (75)
cylindrical (76)	yucca (77)	sotol (77)	ominous (79)

Discussion Questions and Activities

1. What has Madec done to the catch basin? *(Page 69, He has shoveled out the wet sand so that it dries out.)* What does this prove about him? *(It emphasizes his cruelty.)*

2. Why does Ben think the Jeep is so important? *(Page 70, The Jeep provides water, protection, food, movement, communication, weapons, and comfort.)*
3. Which way does Ben choose to walk? *(page 74, west)* How far is it to safety? *(35 miles—see map, Chapter 5.)*
4. Explain the following sentence: "That was all Ben needed to see...where he was going." *(Page 74, Students should understand the significance of the ray of light shining through the butte.)*
5. When is a saguaro cactus full grown? *(page 75, after two hundred years)*
6. Why is Ben happy to see a giant saguaro? *(Pages 75-77, He knows it will contain woodpecker nests which he can use for shoes.)*
7. In what way is the Gila woodpecker smarter than people? *(Page 75, The woodpecker will use the saguaro for a nest but never kill it.)*
8. On page 69, the author uses the idea of a chain holding Ben and Madec together. Why is a chain a good symbol of their situation? What examples have we seen so far of this struggle having "no rules of behavior, no sportsmanship, no gentlemanly conduct." *(examples—making Ben strip, destroying the old man's water can, ruining the catch basin)*
9. Figures of Speech—Similes and Personification:
    a) How are the following phrases examples of personification?
        1) "The whole chain of the Rocky Mountains was vomited upward." (page 71)
        2) "Saguaro...with strong upright praying arms." (page 75)
        3) "The butte...standing silent, and somehow, sullen in the empty desert." (page 79)
    b) Explain the following similes.
        1) "horses...as big as basset hounds..." (page 72)
        2) "...standing like dumb, motionless sentinels." (page 75)
        3) "...looked like long, slim fishing poles." (page 76)
10. **Prediction:** Can Ben make it to the butte before sunrise?

Chapter 7—Pages 81-97

Vocabulary

butte (81)	implacable (81)	stratum (81)	crevice (82)
lassitude (82)	pendulum (86)	abraded (89)	

Discussion Questions and Activities

1. What are the stages of a person dying of thirst? *(page 82, a. loss of strength, lassitude, desire to sleep; b. dizziness, vomiting, headache, ache all over; c. itching, hallucinations)*
2. What is Ben's greatest fear? *(Page 83, Ben fears that he will not recognize the hallucinations; therefore, he can't stop them or continue to think logically.)*
3. Continue your list of chapter titles.

Supplementary Activities

1. Illustrate the main events in Chapter 7 in comic strip form.
2. What is dehydration? How does it occur? What is the treatment for dehydration? Use the library to write a short report on dehydration.
3. Prediction: Will Madec find Ben on the butte?

Chapter 8—Pages 98-106

Vocabulary

hobble (99)   pitons (100)

Discussion Questions and Activities

1. How does Ben know he can't survive much longer? *(Page 98, He has begun to itch, a symptom of the final stage.)*
2. Why does Ben say that he had been cheated, he had been robbed? *(Page 99, After his struggle to get across the wedge-shaped crack, the ledge ends. He cannot go forward and hasn't the strength to return.)*
3. Illustrate Ben's predicament.
4. What does Ben discover at the end of the tunnel? *(Page 106, Ben finds what looks like a clear, sparkling lake.)* Why is this so important?
5. Figures of Speech—Similes and Personification:
   a) Complete the following similes.
      "...the blood stood like ______________________." (page 98)
      "The surface of the rock was as smooth as a ____________________." (page 99)
      "It (Ben's situation) was like a ______________________." (page 99)
   b) Find an example of personification on page 98. ("...the sun, looking small and mean, was frying him.")
6. **Prediction:** Will finding the water really help Ben?

Chapter 9—Pages 107-114

Vocabulary

guano (108)   debris (110)   lethal (111)   covey (112)
plumes (112)

Vocabulary Activities

1. Complete the following analogies. Use the words from Chapter 6 to Chapter 9.
   a) scribble : write—____________ : walk
   b) ____________ : climb—broom : sweep
   c) ____________ : crack—pinnacle : peak
   d) ____________ : stones—alien : foreign
   (Answers: hobble, piton, fissure, breccia)
2. Find the word which does NOT belong in each group.

a. covey	b. guano	c. school	d. pride
a. magma	b. yucca	c. pumice	d. basalt
a. crag	b. mesa	c. sotol	d. pinnacle

   (Answers: guano, yucca, sotol)

Discussion Questions and Activities

1. What usually occurs when people dying of thirst are rescued? *(Page 107, They begin to cry.)* Why is this strange? *(Their eyes are bone dry and crying is painful.)*

2. Describe the lake Ben found? *(Pages 107-108, It is 15 feet in diameter and 2 feet deep, surrounded by bird droppings, murky, stale, with a dusty taste.)*
3. Why would Ben feel hunger now and not earlier? (Refer to stages of thirst.) *(Page 82, A person dying of thirst experiences an odd lack of hunger.)*
4. Why would the light at the ends of the tunnel be different now? *(Pages 108-109, The light indicates the rising and the setting of the sun.)*
5. Change your illustration from Chapter 8, #3 to show Ben's situation now.
6. Draw a picture of the slingshot. *(page 110)*
7. What might be the importance of the slingshot? *(Page 110, He could kill something for food with the slingshot. Both the food and the water would add to his time.)*
8. Where does Ben get the buckshot? *(Page 54, When Ben discovers the slingshot at the old man's campsite, he also finds buckshot.)*
9. Draw a picture of the quail approaching the water. *(page 112)* Have you ever seen a covey of quail? Where? When?
10. How does Ben plan to cook the next birds he kills? *(Page 113, He plans to put them out on the stone in the sun.)* Do you think you could eat raw birds?

Supplementary Activities

1. The quail are unconcerned about their dead companions. Do any birds mate for life? Which kinds? Do other wild animals?
2. What is the recommended amount of water needed per person per day? Why? What does water do for the body's systems?
3. Groups of animals are referred to with different terms. Ben speaks of a "covey of quail." What term is used for sheep, fish, lions? What unusual group names can you discover? Illustrate one or several of these groups.
4. **Prediction:** What enormous thing has Ben been putting out of his mind?

Chapter 10—Pages 115-121

Vocabulary

escarpment (119)   peen (118)   harass (120)

Discussion Questions and Activities

1. What are the voices Ben hears? *(page 115, the voices of the desert in the wind)* Why don't the voices scare him? *(Page 115, His father had told him that the desert had to talk at night because it was so quiet during the day.)*
2. Why didn't Ben ever shave when he went on long trips to the desert? *(Page 116, A beard helped protect his face from the sun.)*
3. Add to your chart of likenesses and differences of Madec and Ben.
4. In this chapter, Ben again speaks of the "chain" between Madec and him. How can he shorten it? Why must he? *(Pages 117-118, Madec will not let Ben escape; therefore, Ben must get close enough to him to force a fair struggle, face to face. "I must either go to him or I must pull him to me.")*
5. What is Madec's plan? *(Pages 118-119, He is climbing the butte to a ledge which leads up to the top. With Madec on the top of the butte, Ben would be trapped.)* Why is it easier for Madec to climb than for Ben? *(Page 120, Madec has tools, steel pegs, and a rope.)*

6. Remember your list of chapter titles.
7. Figures of Speech—Similes and Personification:
    a) Find a simile on page 109. *("...it looked like a great slab of brownish cheese pocked with little holes.")* What is the antecedent of it? *(the tunnel wall)*
    b) Find a simile to describe the helicopter. *(Page 121, "The helicopter was like transparent gold floating in the sky, coming nearer and nearer.")*
    c) Find examples of personification in the description of the quail. *(Page 112, "They were talking to each other in a low, fluty, chatter...little curved plumes...bobbing up and down as though they were nodding agreement.")*
    d) What voices does Ben hear in the wind.? *(Page 115, "...the whispering, the faint dry laughter, the chattering that sometimes sounded insane.")*

Supplementary Activities

1. Read the story of David and Goliath. Compare it to the situation of Ben and Madec.
2. **Prediction:** Will the helicopter rescue Ben?

Chapter 11—Pages 122-130

Vocabulary

stratum (126)   bisected (126)

Discussion Questions and Activities

1. How does Ben know Denny O'Neil is the pilot? *(Pages 122-123, Denny would always keep the helicopter running when he landed in the desert.)*
2. Describe the man with Denny. *(Page 123, He's wearing a purple shirt, yellow trousers, white shoes, and has no hat.)* Why is Ben sure the man isn't Les Stanton? *(Page 123, Les would never wear low-cut white shoes in the desert.)* Why not?
3. Why is it especially insulting to Ben to think of being killed by Madec? *(Page 125, Ben has always lived in the desert. He finds it outrageous to be killed by a man from the city.)*
4. Continue your chart of likenesses and differences.
5. When Madec walks back to the Jeep, what does Ben notice about him? *(Page 129, Ben could tell that Madec was tired.)*

Supplementary Activity

Prediction: What do you think Ben's plan is?

Chapter 12—Pages 131-141

Discussion Questions and Activities

1. Make a chart showing Ben's three possible plans. What was the problem with each one?
   PLANS
   a) Walk to the camp, get the Hornet, and shoot Madec.
   b) Hide behind the rock and nail him with the slingshot as he went to the butte in the morning.
   c) Now that Ben has had water, just take off for home.

   PROBLEMS
   a) Madec might see or hear him coming and shoot him first.
   b) Madec might take another route.
   c) No place to hide during the day, no shoes.
2. Why does Ben walk backward? *(Page 134, so he could brush away the footprints as he went)*
3. What is Ben's plan? *(Pages 136-137, He plans to bury himself in the sand.)* What do you think of this plan? Could you do it?
4 How does Ben use the two tubes from the sling shot? *(Pages 136-137, He puts one in his ear to hear with and the other in his mouth for breathing.)*
5. What fears does Ben have as he waits in the sand? *(Pages 137-139, If too much tubing is exposed, Madec could see it; if too little, the blowing sand might come down the tube, forcing Ben to push his head out.)*

Supplementary Activities

1. Think of a time when you were in a "tight spot," literally or figuratively. Write a paragraph explaining how you got out of it. Be sure to include words that express your feelings at the time.
2. What do you call the feeling some people get when they are closed in? Do you know anybody with this problem? How does he/she cope with it? What are some other phobias people have?
3. **Prediction:** What do you think the sounds are?

Chapter 13—Pages 142-154

Vocabulary

imperceptible (143) obsolete (145)

Discussion Questions and Activities

1. How has Madec foiled Ben's plans? *(Page 151, Madec has the bolt for the rifle, the key and rotor for the Jeep with him.)*
2. How does Ben get Madec to come back from the butte? *(Page 153, Ben sets fire to the tent.)*
3. Who has the upper hand at the end of Chapter 13?
4. Explain how the author uses the idea of a chain to show how Ben's situation changes. (See pages 148, 149, 152.)
5. Continue the list of chapter titles.
6. Figures of Speech—Similes and Personification:
   a) Find an example of personification on page 123. *("And engines are smart. And they're mean.")*
   b) On page 144, find a simile that describes Madec on the wall of the butte. *("He looked like some huge, distorted fly clinging to the rock...")*

Supplementary Activities

1. Make a diagram of Madec and Ben's positions now.
2. **Prediction:** What is Ben's plan now?

Chapter 14—Pages 155-164

Vocabulary

probing [probe] (159) gangrene (162) petty (162) yokel (164)

Discussion Questions and Activities

1. Timeline: put the following items in the correct chronological order.
   A. Ben gets the gun.
   B. Ben gets the keys, bolt, and rotor from Madec's jacket.
   C. Ben puts the rotor in the Jeep.
   D. Ben puts on the old man's clothes and boots.
   E. There is a fire in the tent.
   F. Ben shoots Madec with the slingshot.
   G. Ben ties up Madec.
   H. Ben returns to the butte.
   I. Ben straps Madec into the Jeep.
   (Answers: E, F, A, G, H, B, C, D, I)
2. Page 159 describes Madec staring at Ben. How do you interpret Madec's look—"a steady, cold, intelligent probing"? Why is it not anger, defeat or fear? *(Madec has not given up. He is still sure that he can get out of the situation.)*
3. Before heading back to town, why does Ben stop to get the old man's body? *(Page 159, Ben doesn't want to leave his body in the desert for the vultures to attack.)* What does this tell you about Ben? *(He's conscientious—he wants to do the right thing. He cares about people, even a dead derelict.)*
4. What "jungle" does Madec live in? *(page 162, the business world)*
5. During the conversation in the Jeep many differences show up between Madec and Ben. Add these to your chart. *(Examples—Ben, simple, straightforward, honest; Madec, rich, expert liar, survivor, smart, shrewd, cold.)*
6. Would most poor, college-aged youths accept Madec's offer? Why doesn't Ben? Would you?
7. Figures of Speech—Foreshadowing and Metaphors: Foreshadowing occurs when the reader is given a hint of future action. This chapter contains several examples of foreshadowing. Explain what hints each of the following phrases gives the reader.
   a) Madec's look was one of "steady, cold, intelligent probing." (page 159)
   b) "I'm a liar, Ben." (page 161)
   c) "And I'm a survivor, Ben." (page 162)

   A metaphor is a comparison made without using the words like or as.
   a) Find a metaphor on page 156. *("row of little round hills")* What is being described? *(Madec's knuckles)*

Supplementary Activities

1. A moral dilemma. Think of a time when you or someone you know was faced with a choice between right and wrong. Before you write, consider these questions. What made the choice difficult? Were there rewards attached to either choice? What were the feelings of you/your friend? Did anyone else know about the problem? Did you/your friend discuss this with anyone? How was the problem resolved? Looking back, do you feel it was the correct solution? Now write a paragraph explaining the problem and evaluating this decision.
2. **Prediction:** How will Madec try to put the blame on Ben?

Chapter 15—Pages 165-179

Vocabulary

palo verde (165) haughty (171) abrasions (174) lacerations (174)

Discussion Questions and Activities

1. How does the deputy's reaction to Madec and to the old man differ? *(Page 168, The deputy treats Madec with respect. He immediately calls him Mr., gently helps him out of the Jeep, and gets a car for him. His response to the old man's body is "Ugh!")*
2. How does Madec threaten Ben? *(Page 169, Take the $10,000 or spend 10 years in jail.)* Do you think Madec is that powerful?
3. What two circumstances hurt Ben in this chapter? *(Neither Sergeant Ham nor Dr. Myers is on duty. Ben has confidence in both of them and they are both friendly toward Ben.)*
4. Why does Ben receive such rough treatment from the doctor and the nurse? *(Pages 175-176, They have taken care of Madec first and believe that Ben is responsible for Madec's condition.)*
5. Strick questions Ben about the old prospector's death. How could the old man have been shot more than once? Refer to Chapters 1-2. *(Pages 13-20, Madec shoots the old man with his .358 Magnum. Pages 23-33, Madec shoots the old man with Ben's Hornet.)* Why does Madec shoot him twice? *(Page 33, In case he needs to put the blame on Ben later.)*
6. How does this multiple shooting incriminate Ben? *(Page 177, It makes Ben seem to be unnecessarily cruel.)*
7. **Prediction:** Will anyone believe Ben's version of the story?

Chapter 16—Pages 180-204

Discussion Questions and Activities

1. How might the slingshot have disappeared? *(Page 185, Madec must have taken it somehow.)*
2. Why doesn't Ben's uncle believe him? *(Page 187, Ben's story sounds too bizarre to be true; pages 190-191, Ben's uncle recalls Ben's hot temper.)*
3. What evidence is Ben's best hope of convincing the justice of the peace and the sheriff that he, not Madec, is telling the truth? *(Pages 198-199, the presence of quail bones and a lizard skin. Page 202, Ben can describe the clothing of the men in the helicopter. If he were actually seven miles away, as Madec claims, he never could have seen their clothes.)*
4. How do Mr. Madec's lawyers respond to the evidence? *(Page 199, They make light of Ben's arguments, calling the presence of bones "minor details," and pointing out the rifle's telescopic sight.)*
5. What do you think Ben's feelings are at the end of Chapter 16? *(probably hopelessness and despair)*

6. Write chapter titles in your notebook.
7. **Prediction:** How can Ben prove his innocence?

Chapter 17—Pages 205-220

Vocabulary

forensic (214) pathologist (214) affable (216) collusion (217)

Discussion Questions and Activities

1. How do Mr. Madec's lawyers explain Ben's gun wound? *(Pages 209-210, Mr. Barowitz claims that Ben shot himself.)*
2. The doctor's findings clear Ben. What are the four parts to the doctor's statement? *(Page 213, The larger bullet, the .358, killed the old man. Page 215, The old man was shot by the Hornet bullets an hour later. Page 216, The doctor found buckshot, not a bullet, in Madec's wrist. Page 218, The doctor found the slingshot in the trash.)*
3. Explain the last paragraph on page 219. "Nobody said anything." *(Everyone is too embarrassed to look at Ben. They had been willing to believe Madec instead of him.)*
4. Explain Ben's last statement on page 220. Why wouldn't he want to press charges? Should he?
5. Is the ending satisfying? Would the ending have been better if Mr. Madec were convicted and imprisoned? Why? Why not?

Supplementary Activity

Crossword #2 could be assigned now. (See page 28 of this guide.)

Post-reading Activities

1. Debate the Topic: Ben should have accepted Madec's proposal.
2. Chapter Titles: Make a booklet of the chapter titles you wrote during the reading. Illustrate each chapter. This assignment could be done as a class assignment, one chapter per student, or as a small group project.
3. Timeline: arrange the following events in the correct chronological order.
   - A. An old man is killed.
   - B. Ben uses woodpecker nests for shoes.
   - C. Ben kills some quail for food.
   - D. Ben buries himself in the sand.
   - E. Ben finds a slingshot.
   - F. Ben sets fire to the tent.
   - G. Ben discovers the catch basin is destroyed.
   - H. Madec begins to climb the butte.
   - I. The helicopter lands in the desert.
   - J. Ben finds a "lake" on the butte.
   - K. No one believes Ben's story.
   - L. The doctor proves Ben's innocence.

   (Answers: A, E, G, B, J, C, H, I, D, F, K, L)

4. Design and write the articles for the first page of the local paper to be published the day after these events. The lead story should tell of Ben and Madec's encounter. Other articles might include a background story of the desert area involved, a feature on Madec and his business, an interview with Ben, the weather summary, ads, sports update, etc. Be sure to give your paper a title. This might be good work for a group, rather than an individual.
5. Construct a diorama of a desert scene. Include desert plants and animals as well as land forms such as mountains, buttes, rocks, etc.
6. Use your chart of the likenesses and differences between Ben and Madec to write a paper describing either character. Choose a few of his most important qualities and give examples of each one. Use the character's speech, actions or thoughts for your examples.
7. Library Research:
   a) Make a list of at least five books relating to mountain climbing. Write the title, author, publisher, place of publication, and date of publication. The books may be either fiction or non-fiction. Use either your school library or the public library. Check out the book that sounds the most interesting.
   b) Make a list of five magazine articles about hiking in the desert. Write the title and author of the article, the name, date, and volume number of the periodical. To find this information, use the *Readers' Guide to Periodical Literature.*
   c) Using an almanac, make a list of five deserts of the United States. Tell the location and the approximate size of each. Possible answers might include:

Desert	Location	Square Miles
Black Rock	NV	1,000
Chihuahuan	TX, NM, AZ, Mexico	140,000
Death Valley	CA, NV	3,000
Mojave	CA, AZ	15,000
Painted Desert	AZ	200
Sonoran	AZ, CA, Mexico	70,000

   d) What is the largest desert in the world? *(Sahara)* How large is it? *(3,500,000 sq. mi.)*
   e) Name the highest mountain in the United States. Give its location and height. *(Mt. McKinley, Alaska; 20,320 ft.)*
   f) What is the highest mountain in the world? *(Mt. Everest)* What mountain range is it in? *(Himalayas)* How high is it? *(29,028 ft.)*
   g) What almanac did you use to find the information on deserts and mountains? Give the name and date of the almanac.
8. The author uses the chain as a symbol of the connections between Ben and Madec. Why is this a good symbol? Reread pages 69, 117, 148, 149, 152. Then write a paper about how the chain is used as a symbol and how the symbol develops throughout the story.
9. If you enjoyed this book, you might like to read two other books of survival. Look for *Alive* by Paul Read and *Endurance* by Alfred Lansing.

Desert Animals Word Search Puzzle

Words can be found vertically, horizontally, diagonally, backwards or forwards.

```
A J R K T V B E D E P I T N E C B J T R G O
S C E N I N O I L N I A T N U O M A H E R X
K P A L L S P Q G C B R A G U O C C T T O Z
A V A S F B S E N H S R M H Q G D K H S U D
N F L R W O P B Q F O B J K P I R R D N N Z
G U Q I R H W Z U A Y R A O A L A A E O D D
A K I T F O X L D G H Y N A Z A Z B S M S A
R K S U Y P W R O S K K I L G W I B E A Q O
O H G T W N U H E R U T L U V O L I R L U T
O S E K A N S L A R O C E T S O L T T I I T
R O K S N P L G A W A I V N P D I L M G R O
A T O E G E S E G M K O A A I P A B U R R O
T F R W N Z W F L I E S J R D E T C L B E F
E I E J A E E T O Y O C P A E C P N E O L E
G O D E I R I A R P J Z S T R K I Q D B V D
V R G A M B E L S Q U A I L L E H E E C Z A
H O R N E D T O A D U V A K N R W P E A R P
T O R T O I S E I N O I P R O C S O R T T S
```

COUGAR
BURRO
SPIDER
GILAWOODPECKER
SPADEFOOTTOAD
BOBCAT
SPARROWHAWK
HORNEDTOAD
TARANTULA

JACKRABBIT
KITFOX
VULTURE
ROADRUNNER
JAVELINA
GAMBELSQUAIL
GROUNDSQUIRREL
GILAMONSTER

CENTIPEDE
COYOTE
PRAIRIEDOG
DESERTMULEDEER
EWE
KANGAROORAT
ANT
CORALSNAKE

BIGHORN
FLIES
ELFOWL
SCORPION
TORTOISE
MOUNTAINLION
WHIPTAILLIZARD
KISSBUG

Desert Plants and Trees Word Search Puzzle

Words can be found vertically, horizontally, diagonally, backwards or forwards.

D N I G H T B L O O M I N G C E R E U S M D
O X A H J D E E W E L B M U T D P I Q U T M
E R Z N Q B N V S X Q G S E J A R L M F B Q
X J G L E F E Q C J Q U K T L Y I S A K N U
K M N A V B U A C E T T C O T R C A G C N V
S K J V N I R O V C A B V S H R K G U N S D
Q U Z U T P P E A E Y E G O R E L E E A R O
B I T E M G I C V C R G B E E B Y U Y Z Y M
Q A W P E P O P A D W T R R A K P O C M L M
R X R D Y R I E E C N O A C D C E N R I C K
P E B R A L T N E C C A H I P A A R T K Q A
D B E U E G A D G R A U S B L H R O T K M P
M J G R X L A C O C T C Y E A C C H U Q D E
H A L R T R C V U O H A T K N O A K M E O T
S O T O L E W A E E W O U U T W C C J E A A
N N Y M X J K M C A Q N L H S E T U T D Y D
F A N P A L M O Y T W K O L S E U B J U L J
A I L E C N E Y M Z U T B R A O S X O A S T
B O T T L E B R U S H S J Q I D J W C N S R

SAGUAROCACTUS
BARRELCACTUS
MESQUITE
YUCCA
SOTOL
PALOVERDE
PRICKLYPEARCACTUS
JUMPINGCHOLLA
NIGHTBLOOMINGCEREUS
DATEPALM
EUCALYPTUS
JOSHUATREE
OCOTILLO
SMOKETREE
CATSCLAW
TUMBLEWEED
CREOSOTE
ORGANPIPECACTUS
BEAVERTAILCACTUS
FANPALM
AGAVE
MESCAL
MAGUEY
IRONWOODTREE
HACKBERRY
SANDVERBENA
ENCELIA
THREADPLANT
BOTTLEBRUSH
SAGE
MILKWOOD
BUCKHORN

Desert Forms and Rocks Word Search Puzzle

Words can be found vertically, horizontally, diagonally, backwards or forwards.

A A H P C U R B U J P I A O Z S Q E N K H R N B M
E H Y I K K P J U E C C A H L M K O V M A G M A G
A O R N H E I D X T C G Q A H E A V E G A E Y O S
C M P N M Y Z G P N T I B W E T L W R Z I S I H R
Q S S A O I V E Y C O E M E N S P C P C C Y F A Q
Q Q B C T F C B J B K R D U R M C D C N C T I B F
H U J L P K A C G O I D O I P U Q A H J E F Q K M
A S A E K S A A O U O M R E H T S P R E R W Q Z Q
K C H R I Y C V D L T P E G D E L S O P B R J Z H
Z J P N T P Y O W D J E E B T Q H J O T M U G L S
E L A H S Z S P H E R B P H E Y F J F F L E O E V
O Z G S O G Q A U R I B I H R W O F Z B N O N E W
E C H L Y A F S E F D L D Z R P I O A H E E N T S
Z D O O O R C E R D S E R G A L A S E Q V H B U J
H E U P R C Z M K Y N J M B C T A H G Q M A M R C
N K D E R W U A E T A L P D E L N L D P P M H U S
S V U F A W K E G F M F K Z T Z T G I N I A D V C
H N T M R M Z B L R Y D B W P Q T P R T U A K P B

SHALE
BRECCIA
MOUNTAIN
QUARTZ
ARROYO
LEDGE
PUMICE

BUTTE
MESA
TERRACE
SLOPE
SLAB
PINNACLE

PLATEAU
BASIN
BASALT
ESCARPMENT
RIDGE
CRAG

CLIFF
PEBBLE
FISSURE
BOULDER
MAGMA
SUMMIT

Vocabulary Crossword Puzzle, Chapters 1-6

ACROSS

6. Holding fast
7. Foreign
9. Guard
11. Dry gully
12. Steep, rugged rock or cliff
13. Shaking
16. 5-gallon water container
21. Common mineral
22. Person unable to support himself
23. Lily-like plant with stiff, sharp-pointed leaves
24. Threatening
26. Being on guard against danger
27. High, pointed peak
28. Molten rock

DOWN

1. Plant resembling a yucca
2. Primp
3. Small plateau with steep sides
4. Volcanic glass
5. Full, unobstructed view
8. Possibility
10. Cut
14. Isolated hill with steep sides
15. Sharp fragments of rock
17. Side sheltered from wind
18. Spread throughout
19. Narrow opening or crack in a rock
20. Rate of motion
25. Female sheep

Vocabulary Crossword Puzzle, Chapters 7-17

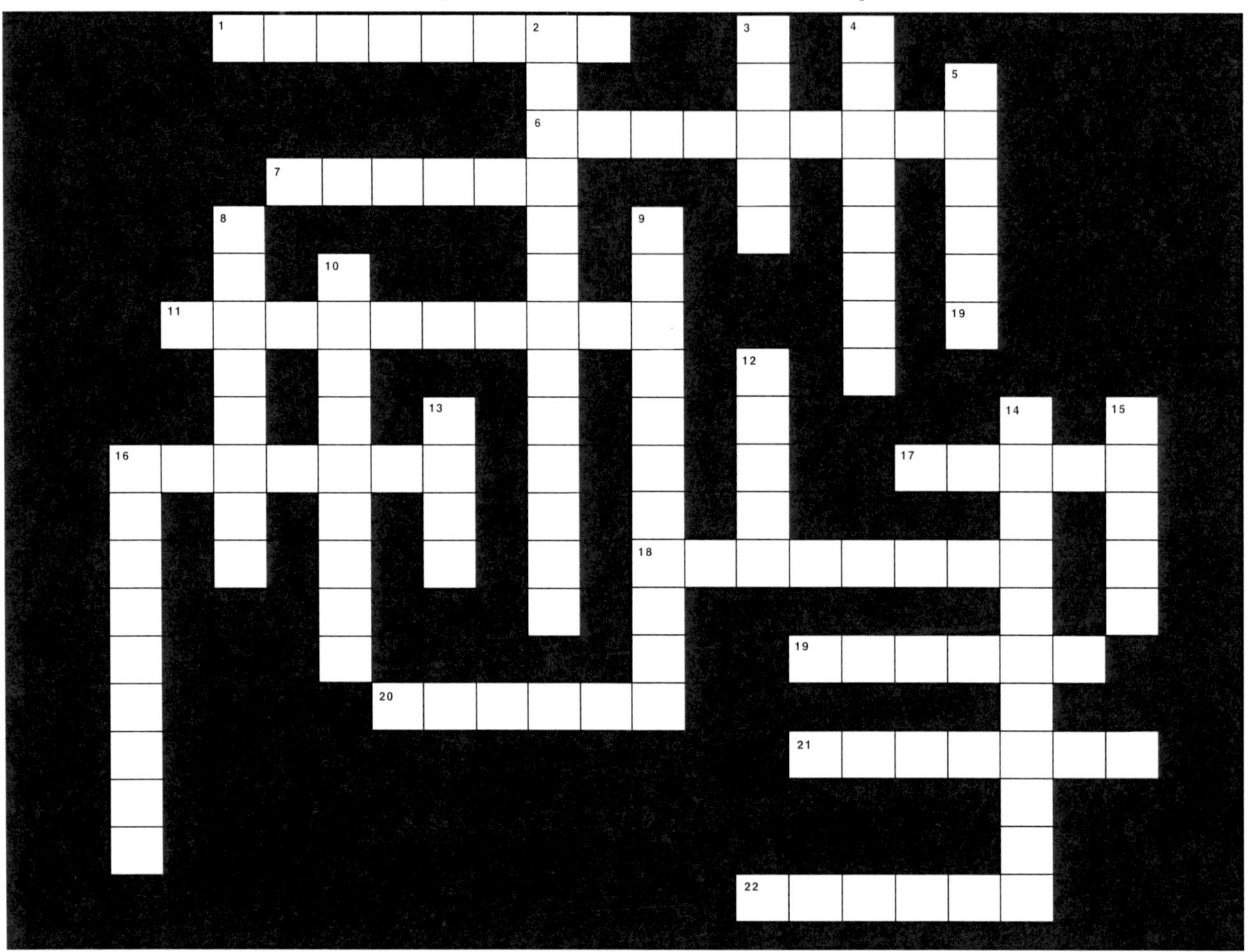

ACROSS	DOWN
1. Suitable to courts of law	2. Too slight to notice
6. Desert tree with green branches	3. Small flock of birds
7. Walk with difficulty	4. Place where surface has been rubbed away
11. Long cliff	5. Accumulation of fragments of rock
16. Narrow opening caused by split or crack	8. No longer in use
17. Seabird excrement used as fertilizer	9. One who studies diseases
18. Death of tissue due to loss of blood	10. Weariness, fatigue
19. Capable of causing death	12. Spike driven into rock for support
20. Divide into two equal parts	13. Wedged-shaped end of hammer
21. Searching examination	14. Torn or ragged wounds
22. Tire out by persistent efforts	15. Rustic, bumpkin
	16. Secret agreement

Puzzle Answers

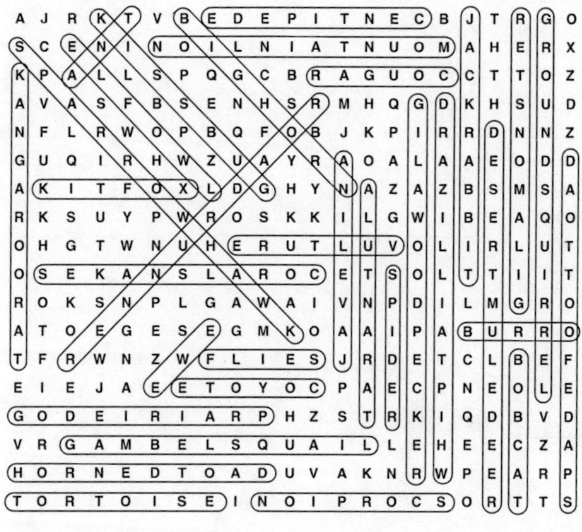

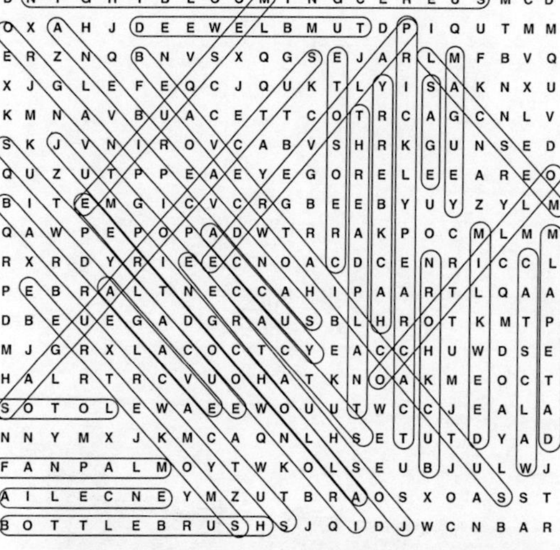

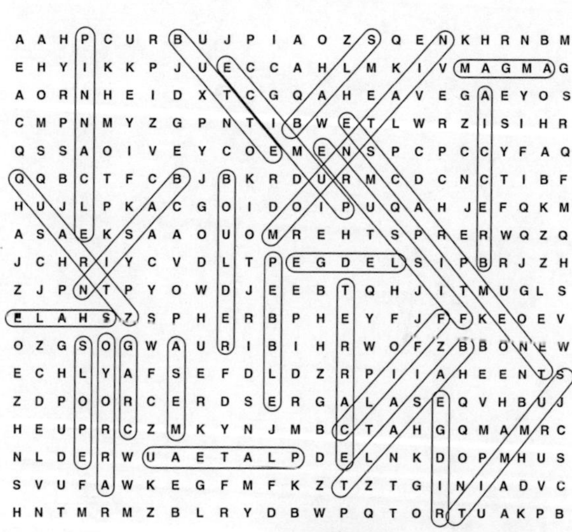

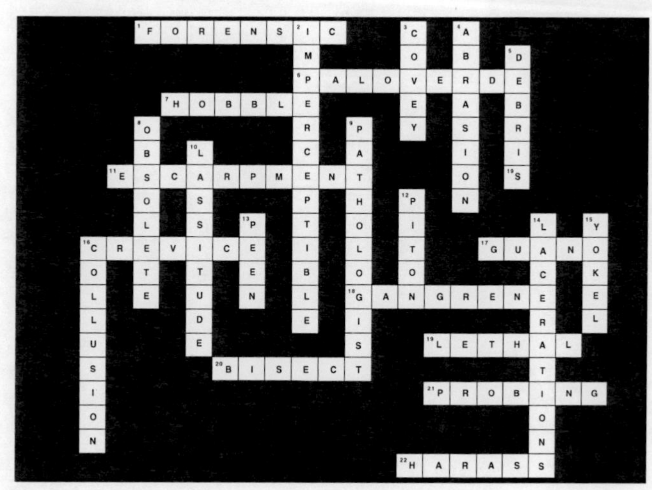

Notes

Notes

Notes